Quick & Healthy

Quick & Healthy

50
Simple,
Delicious Recipes for Every Day

American Cancer Society®

Published by the American Cancer Society,
250 Williams Street NW, Atlanta, GA 30303-1002

Printed in Canada

Recipe Development by Nancy S. Hughes

Photography by Valerie Iliff

Nutritional Analysis by Madelyn L. Wheeler, MS, RD

Design and Composition by Lisa Sparer

5 4 3 2 1   20 21 22 23 24

Library of Congress Cataloging-in-Publication Data is available.

For more information about cancer, contact your American Cancer Society at **800-227-2345** or visit **cancer.org**. For inquiries about our books, quantity discounts, or other information, e-mail **trade.sales@cancer.org**.

Recipe shown on cover: Turkey & Red Cabbage Tortillas with Chipotle Sauce, page 17

Contents

Recipes

Chicken and Turkey

Seafood

Introduction

THERE IS MORE SCIENTIFIC EVIDENCE NOW THAN EVER BEFORE THAT THE CHOICES WE MAKE about what we eat are tied to our risk for cancer and other chronic diseases—from heart disease to diabetes to arthritis. Yet, it can be challenging to make good food choices when you are balancing a busy schedule and the demands of life.

As part of the American Cancer Society's mission to save lives, we want to share what we know about nutrition to help you make better choices for your family and live a healthier and longer life. Studies have shown that people who cook often at home eat better—less sugar, less fat, fewer refined carbohydrates, and less food in general—than people who cook less frequently or not at all. When you cook at home, you are in control of what you buy, how it's prepared, and how much you eat.

Quick & Healthy: 50 Simple, Delicious Recipes for Every Day is designed to make cooking at home easier by providing you with healthy main dish recipes that are as delicious as they are simple. Using a few ingredients, anyone can put together a nutritious meal in less time than it would take to order delivery. Plus, the recipes call for common, easy-to-find ingredients, so you can get started right away.

Here's the simple truth: Eating well is an important part of improving your health and lowering your risk of disease, and it is an important part of feeling your best *every* day. The American Cancer Society's nutritional guidelines focus on four key points:

➤ Choose foods and drinks in amounts that help you get to and maintain a healthy weight.
➤ Limit how much processed meat and red meat you eat.
➤ Eat at least 2½ cups of vegetables and fruits each day.
➤ Choose whole grains instead of refined grain products.

The healthiest diets share these things in common: a lot of vegetables, fruits, whole grains, legumes, and nuts; moderate amounts of low-fat and nonfat dairy products and alcohol; and low intake of red and processed meats, sugar-sweetened foods and drinks, and refined carbohydrates.

Portion control is another essential component of a healthy diet, but it can be easier in principle than in practice. Average portion sizes are 2 to 5 times as big as they were in the past. For example, 20 years ago, a regular serving of French fries weighed 2.4 ounces and had 210 calories. Today's typical serving of fries is a whopping 6.9 ounces and 610 calories. That's important because research shows most people eat and drink more when served more.

For many of us, the first step to being more mindful of portion size is simply to remind ourselves of standard serving sizes. Look at the chart below.

FOOD		VISUAL CUE
1 cup broccoli	=	Baseball
Potato	=	Computer mouse
Medium apple or orange	=	Tennis ball
½ cup chopped or cooked fruit	=	Computer mouse
½ cup brown rice	=	Computer mouse
1 cup pasta or dry cereal	=	Fist (with fingers tucked in)
2-3 ounces cooked meat, poultry, or fish	=	Deck of cards
2 tablespoons peanut butter	=	Ping pong ball
¼ cup dried fruit	=	Ping pong ball

How do those serving sizes compare with what you might have thought otherwise? How does this compare to what you might receive at a restaurant or serve yourself at home?

We all want to eat food we enjoy, food that is healthy and makes us feel good. This book will help you do that. So let's get started.

If you're not in the habit of cooking at home, there are some simple ways to make home cooking easier:

➤ Start gradually. Make dinner once or twice a week and work your way up from there.

➤ Keep your kitchen and pantry organized and stocked with staples so that you can put together a meal quickly. If things are easy to find, it will shorten prep time.

➤ Plan! Schedule time to plan the week's meals. Some people do this on the weekend, some do it Monday morning once the kids are off to school—do whatever works with your schedule. This will save you time and money.

➤ Before you start cooking, read through the recipe to get a sense of what's involved.

➤ Take shortcuts! For example, studies have shown that frozen vegetables are just as nutritious as fresh and are a huge timesaver (just steer clear of frozen veggies with added sauces or seasonings). Fresh salsas and good-quality tomato sauces (without added sugars) are also ingredients that can add flavor and speed prep time.

➤ If you are using prepared foods, choose and use them smartly. Read labels and avoid products with added sugars, high levels of sodium, or high levels of unhealthy fats.

Remember, also, recipes aren't written in stone—they should be used as guides. If you don't like an ingredient, use less, leave it out, or choose a substitute. If there's something you love, add a bit more. Some recipes list optional ingredients—they will enhance the flavor and look of the dish, but are *not* essential! Take them or leave them—it's entirely up to you.

Every recipe is accompanied by a beautiful color photo to inspire you, along with a helpful tip and nutritional information. Keep these things in mind as you use that information:

➤ The nutrition information shown is for one serving.
➤ Ingredients that are optional or listed without a specific amount are not included in the analysis.
➤ When a choice of ingredients is given, the first option was used in the analysis.
➤ All data are rounded according to the U.S. Food and Drug Administration Rounding Rules.

Above all, enjoy yourself! Cooking doesn't have to be a chore. Don't be afraid to try something new or be creative. The simpler the preparation, the easier it is for fresh and flavorful ingredients to shine through. So take this book and have fun—it can be surprising how much flavor you can get from just a few ingredients and a little time. These recipes will prove quick and healthy—and most importantly, delicious!

Chicken & Turkey

Greens & Grilled Chicken Salad with Creamy Cumin Dressing

This dressing couldn't be any simpler—just sour cream and cumin—but it's the perfect touch to this mouthwatering chicken salad with fresh salsa and creamy avocado.

SERVES 4

- 4 (4-ounce) boneless, skinless chicken breasts, flattened to an even thickness
- Salt and freshly ground black pepper
- ½ cup reduced-fat sour cream
- ¼ cup water
- ½ teaspoon ground cumin
- 6 cups torn green leaf or romaine lettuce
- 1 cup fresh salsa
- 1 avocado, pitted and chopped

1. Heat a grill or grill pan to medium-high heat. Coat the grill rack and both sides of the chicken breasts with cooking spray. Season with salt and pepper. Cook chicken 4 to 6 minutes on each side, or until no longer pink in center. Place on cutting board and cool slightly before slicing.

2. Meanwhile, stir together the sour cream, water, and cumin in a large bowl. Toss with the lettuce until well coated and add salt and pepper to taste. Top with the chicken, salsa, and avocado.

Cook's Note For an even healthier recipe, you can substitute nonfat Greek yogurt for the sour cream.

PER SERVING

Calories: 250
Fat: 11 g
Saturated fat: 3.5 g
Cholesterol: 75 mg
Sodium: 105 mg
Carbohydrate: 9 g
Dietary fiber: 4 g
Sugars: 4 g
Protein: 28 g

Balsamic-Red Wine Chicken & Mushrooms

This aromatic dish features chicken smothered with mushrooms, a concentrated wine sauce, and a scattering of melted mozzarella. A "company-worthy" dish for sure!

SERVES 4

- 4 (4-ounce) boneless, skinless chicken breasts, flattened to an even thickness
- Salt and freshly ground black pepper
- 1 (8-ounce) package sliced cremini mushrooms
- ½ cup chopped green onions, divided use
- ⅔ cup red wine
- 3 tablespoons balsamic vinegar
- ½ cup shredded part-skim mozzarella cheese

PER SERVING

Calories: 200
Fat: 5 g
Saturated fat: 2 g
Cholesterol: 75 mg
Sodium: 150 mg
Carbohydrate: 6 g
Dietary fiber: 0.5 g
Sugars: 3 g
Protein: 29 g

1. Preheat oven to 400 degrees.

2. Coat chicken with cooking spray and season with salt and pepper. Heat a large nonstick skillet over medium-high heat. Cook chicken on one side for 3 minutes or until lightly browned. Place, browned side up, in a 2-quart baking dish coated with cooking spray.

3. Place mushrooms and ⅓ cup of the green onions in the skillet, coat lightly with cooking spray, and cook 4 minutes, or until mushrooms begin to brown on edges, stirring occasionally. Spoon evenly over chicken.

4. Add the wine and vinegar to the skillet. Bring to a boil over medium-high heat; boil 3 minutes or until reduced to ¼ cup liquid. Spoon over chicken, season with salt and pepper, and top with the cheese. Bake, uncovered, for 22 to 25 minutes, or until chicken is no longer pink in center. Sprinkle with the remaining green onions. Let stand 5 minutes to absorb flavors.

 Cook's Note To brown the cheese lightly, place under broiler for one minute before topping with the remaining green onion.

Sheet Pan Chicken & Veggies with Horseradish Sour Cream

This sheet pan recipe seasons itself naturally! At the end of roasting, the ingredients are sealed in the foil on which they were cooked, allowing the natural juices to release.

SERVES 4

- 4 (4-ounce) boneless, skinless chicken thighs, rinsed and patted dry
- 1 pound small or "baby" Yukon gold potatoes, about 1 inch in diameter
- 1 medium onion, cut into ½-inch wedges
  Paprika, optional
- 8 ounces whole green beans, ends trimmed and dried well
- ½ cup reduced-fat sour cream
- 1 tablespoon prepared horseradish
  Salt and freshly ground black pepper

PER SERVING

Calories: 220
Fat: 5 g
Saturated fat: 2.5 g
Cholesterol: 70 mg
Sodium: 370 mg
Carbohydrate: 12 g
Dietary fiber: 1 g
Sugars: 10 g
Protein: 28 g

1. Place a foil-lined sheet pan in the oven, making sure the foil is overlapping the edges of the pan slightly. Preheat oven to 425 degrees.

2. Once the oven has preheated, coat the chicken, potatoes, and onion with cooking spray. Sprinkle the smooth side of the chicken with paprika, if desired, and place (smooth side down) on sheet pan. Arrange the potatoes and onions around the chicken in a single layer. Bake 10 minutes and remove pan from oven. Move chicken and vegetables to one side of the pan and turn the chicken over. Add green beans in a single layer, coat with cooking spray, and cook 15 minutes, or until internal temperature of chicken reaches 165 degrees. Remove from oven. Season with salt and pepper.

3. Pull the ends of the foil up and seal. Let stand 10 minutes.

4. Meanwhile, combine the sour cream and horseradish in a small bowl. Season with salt and pepper. Serve dipping sauce alongside chicken and vegetables.

 Cook's Note If the potatoes are larger than an inch in diameter, cut them in half before cooking for even doneness. It's important that they be similar in size.

Apricot-Glazed Chicken on Toasted Nut Quinoa

Quinoa, pronounced "keen-wah," is considered to be a protein-packed grain, but it's actually a seed. To incorporate it into your daily cooking, use it as you would couscous or bulgur, or combine it with other grains. It's fun to experiment! A word of caution: if you need to drain the quinoa, be sure to use a fine mesh sieve, otherwise it will slip through the larger holes and go down the drain!

SERVES 4

- 1 cup quinoa
- ½ cup unsalted peanuts or slivered almonds
- 4 (4-ounce) boneless, skinless chicken breasts, flattened to an even thickness
  Salt and freshly ground black pepper
- ¼ cup apricot fruit spread
- ½ cup water
- 1 tablespoon apple cider vinegar
- 1 teaspoon grated ginger
- ¼ cup chopped fresh cilantro, optional

PER SERVING

Calories: 430
Fat: 14 g
Saturated fat: 2.5 g
Cholesterol: 65 mg
Sodium: 65 mg
Carbohydrate: 43 g
Dietary fiber: 5 g
Sugars: 12 g
Protein: 34 g

1. Cook quinoa according to package directions.

2. Meanwhile, heat a large nonstick skillet over medium-high heat. Add the peanuts and cook 2 minutes or until just beginning to brown, stirring frequently. Set aside on separate plate.

3. Coat both sides of the chicken breasts with nonstick cooking spray and season with salt and pepper. Cook 4 to 6 minutes on each side or until no longer pink in center.

4. Toss the quinoa with the peanuts and season with salt and pepper. Top with the chicken and cover to keep warm.

5. In the same skillet, combine the fruit spread, water, and vinegar over medium-high heat. Bring to a boil and cook 2 minutes, or until reduced to ¼ cup liquid, scraping bottom and sides of skillet as it cooks. Remove from heat, stir in the ginger, and spoon evenly over the chicken. Sprinkle with cilantro, if desired.

 Cook's Note When buying fresh ginger, you do not have to buy a large piece. Simply break off a smaller piece.

Chicken Soup with Fire-Roasted Tomatoes & Hominy

The longer hominy simmers, the more its flavors penetrate into the other ingredients, adding a mellow "tamale" or "corn tortilla" flavor to the dish.

SERVES 4

12 ounces boneless, skinless chicken breast, cut into bite-size pieces
1 (16-ounce) can hominy, rinsed and drained
1 (14.5-ounce) can fire-roasted diced tomatoes with garlic
3 cups water
¼ teaspoon ground chipotle
½ cup chopped fresh cilantro
1 avocado, pitted and chopped
1 lime, quartered, optional

1. Coat a large saucepan with cooking spray and place over medium heat. Add the chicken and cook 2 minutes, stirring occasionally. Add the hominy, tomatoes, water, and ground chipotle and bring to a boil over high heat. Reduce heat and simmer, uncovered, for 25 minutes.

2. Remove from heat, stir in cilantro, and serve topped with avocado. Serve with lime wedges, if desired.

 Cook's Note

If you're not a cilantro fan, you can substitute chopped green onion in this particular dish.

PER SERVING

Calories: 240
Fat: 9 g
Saturated fat: 1.5 g
Cholesterol: 50 mg
Sodium: 410 mg
Carbohydrate: 20 g
Dietary fiber: 6 g
Sugars: 4 g
Protein: 21 g

Skillet Turkey Shepherd's Pie

An old-time favorite can return to your kitchen without hours of work...and with a bit of a twist! Adding chili powder gives a heartiness and richness to the whole dish, and using turkey instead of beef keeps things on the healthy side. Adding the cheese near the end keeps it creamy. Just dig in...you'll see how good it can be.

SERVES 4

- 5 cups water, divided use
- 1 pound red potatoes, cut into ½-inch cubes
- 1 pound ground turkey breast
- 1 (10-ounce) package frozen mixed vegetables (about 2 ½ cups)
- 1 tablespoon chili powder
  Salt and freshly ground black pepper
- 1 cup 2 percent milk
- ¾ cup shredded reduced-fat sharp cheddar cheese

1. Bring 4 cups of the water to a boil in a large saucepan. Add the potatoes, return to a boil, and boil 12 minutes or until very tender.

2. Meanwhile, heat a large nonstick skillet over medium-high heat. Add turkey and cook until browned, stirring frequently. Stir in vegetables, the remaining 1 cup water, and chili powder and bring to a boil. Reduce heat, cover, and simmer 8 minutes or until vegetables are tender. Remove from heat and season with salt and pepper.

3. Remove potatoes from heat and drain well. Return potatoes to the saucepan and mash with a potato masher or electric mixer. Add the milk and continue to mash until well blended. (You may need to add more milk to achieve the desired consistency.) Season with salt and pepper. Spoon evenly over the turkey mixture and sprinkle with cheese. Cover and place over low heat for 10 minutes, or until heated through and cheese melts.

PER SERVING

Calories: 360
Fat: 9 g
Saturated fat: 4 g
Cholesterol: 85 mg
Sodium: 280 mg
Carbohydrate: 32 g
Dietary fiber: 6 g
Sugars: 7 g
Protein: 41 g

Cook's Note

This dish is great the next day, too!

Warm Balsamic Chicken Salad with Blue Cheese

This is not your run-of-the-mill "chicken-on-lettuce" salad. Quick-marinated chicken is grilled, placed over greens, and topped with a still-warm dressing of balsamic vinegar, Worcestershire sauce, and a touch of sugar. A sprinkling of blue cheese finishes it off. See? Definitely not just chicken on lettuce!

SERVES 4

- 4 (4-ounce) boneless, skinless chicken breasts, flattened to an even thickness
- 2 tablespoons sugar
- ¼ cup balsamic vinegar
- 2 tablespoons Worcestershire sauce
- ⅓ cup water
- Salt and freshly ground black pepper
- 6 cups baby spinach
- ½ cup reduced-fat crumbled blue cheese

1. Place chicken in a shallow pan. Whisk together the sugar, vinegar, Worcestershire sauce, and water in a small bowl. Spoon 2 tablespoons of the vinegar mixture over the chicken and turn several times to coat, reserving the remaining vinegar mixture. Season with salt and pepper. Let stand 30 minutes or cover and refrigerate overnight.

2. Heat a nonstick skillet over medium-high heat. Coat both sides of chicken with cooking spray and cook 3 minutes on each side, or until no longer pink in center. Place on cutting board and thinly slice.

3. Add the reserved vinegar mixture to pan residue in skillet, stirring to release any browned bits. Bring to a boil over medium-high heat and boil 2 minutes, or until reduced to ¼ cup liquid.

4. Place the spinach on a serving platter or large bowl and top with the chicken. Drizzle the vinegar mixture over and sprinkle with the cheese.

PER SERVING

Calories: 220

Fat: 5 g

Saturated fat: 2.5 g

Cholesterol: 70 mg

Sodium: 370 mg

Carbohydrate: 12 g

Dietary fiber: 1 g

Sugars: 10 g

Protein: 28 g

 Cook's Note You can replace the spinach with any type of lettuce, preferably a more "assertive" type, such as escarole or a kale mix.

Turkey & Red Cabbage Tortillas with Chipotle Sauce

They're bright, they're pretty, and they're packed with flavor in every bite. The smoky chipotle pepper penetrates the dish with just a hint of heat! Using ground turkey breast makes this a very lean dish...but definitely not lean on flavor.

SERVES 4

- 8 corn tortillas
- 1 pound ground turkey breast
- 1 teaspoon ground chipotle, divided use
  Salt and freshly ground black pepper
- ½ cup reduced-fat sour cream or Greek yogurt
- 1 cup shredded red cabbage
- ½ cup chopped fresh cilantro

1. Heat a large nonstick skillet over medium-high heat and coat both sides of the tortillas with nonstick cooking spray. Working in batches, cook tortillas 1 minute on each side or until just beginning to brown. Set aside and cover to keep warm. Repeat with remaining tortillas.

2. Add the turkey to the skillet with ½ teaspoon of the ground chipotle and season with salt and pepper. Cook until browned, stirring frequently and breaking up larger pieces while cooking.

3. Meanwhile, stir together the sour cream and the remaining ½ teaspoon ground chipotle in a small bowl. Add salt and pepper to taste.

4. Spoon equal amounts of the turkey mixture onto each tortilla and top with the sour cream mixture, shredded cabbage, and cilantro.

Lightly browning the tortillas brings out the roasted corn flavor, and covering them keeps them soft and pliable until served.

PER SERVING

Calories: 310

Fat: 7 g

Saturated fat: 3 g

Cholesterol: 75 mg

Sodium: 95 mg

Carbohydrate: 28 g

Dietary fiber: 4 g

Sugars: 3 g

Protein: 34 g

Chicken & Red Grape Salad

Break away from the chicken salad humdrum and toss together this slightly sweet curry salad instead. Chilling it a few hours lets the curry take over, giving the creamy salad a soft yellow hue. Serve as is or spoon onto twelve Bibb lettuce leaves for mini wraps. This is also delicious served on raisin bread.

SERVES 4

- ²/₃ cup 2 percent plain Greek yogurt
- 1 tablespoon curry powder
- 1 tablespoon sugar
- 2 cups chopped cooked chicken breast
- 1 ⅓ cups red seedless grapes, halved
- ½ cup finely chopped red onion
  Salt and freshly ground black pepper

1. Combine the yogurt, curry powder, and sugar in a medium bowl. Stir until well blended. Gently stir in the remaining ingredients. Season with salt and pepper.

2. Cover and refrigerate 3 hours to let the flavors meld.

 Cook's Note This recipe is a great way to use up leftover rotisserie chicken.

PER SERVING
Calories: 210
Fat: 3.5 g
Saturated fat: 1 g
Cholesterol: 60 mg
Sodium: 70 mg
Carbohydrate: 17 g
Dietary fiber: 1 g
Sugars: 14 g
Protein: 26 g

Thick & Chunky Italian Turkey Soup

If you're tired, cold, and hungry, this is the soup for you. This hearty turkey soup is jam-packed with tomatoes, green beans, pasta, and herbs and served with grated Parmesan. As an added bonus, it thickens and tastes even better the next day!

SERVES 4

1	pound lean ground turkey
1	(14.5-ounce) can stewed tomatoes
2	ounces whole grain rotini pasta (about ⅔ cup uncooked)
4	ounces green beans, trimmed and broken in half
4	cups water
2	tablespoons tomato paste
1½	tablespoons dried oregano
	Salt and freshly ground black pepper
¼	cup grated Parmesan cheese

1. Heat a large saucepan coated with cooking spray over medium-high heat. Add the turkey and cook until browned, stirring frequently and breaking up the larger pieces as it cooks.

2. Add all the remaining ingredients except the cheese and bring to a boil. Reduce heat and simmer, uncovered, for 20 minutes, or until thickened slightly. Break up larger pieces of tomato, if desired. Season with salt and pepper.

3. Serve topped with Parmesan cheese.

 Cook's Note The rotini can be replaced with macaroni, penne, or broken spaghetti noodles.

PER SERVING

Calories: 300
Fat: 10 g
Saturated fat: 3.5 g
Cholesterol: 90 mg
Sodium: 390 mg
Carbohydrate: 23 g
Dietary fiber: 4 g
Sugars: 7 g
Protein: 27 g

Chicken-Sweet Potato Skewers with Sweet & Spicy Sauce

Have you ever tried to thread a green onion on a skewer? "Folding" the green onion is a simple technique for grilling; it keeps them in place while they cook the same amount of time as the other ingredients. This dish is easy, colorful, delicious, and has fantastic visual appeal! You can up the amount of horseradish if you want a spicier sauce.

SERVES 4

4 cups water
1 pound sweet potatoes, peeled and cut into 1-inch cubes (about 32 cubes)
8 chicken tenderloins (about 1 ¼ pounds total), rinsed and patted dry, cut into fourths
24 green onions, trimmed to 6 inches (white and pale green part only)
Salt and freshly ground black pepper
¼ cup apricot fruit spread
¼ cup drained crushed pineapple (reserving 2 tablespoons juice)
1 tablespoon prepared horseradish

PER SERVING
Calories: 290
Fat: 3.5 g
Saturated fat: 1 g
Cholesterol: 80 mg
Sodium: 120 mg
Carbohydrate: 33 g
Dietary fiber: 4 g
Sugars: 17 g
Protein: 32 g

1. Bring water to a boil in a large saucepan over high heat. Carefully add the potatoes and return to a boil. Reduce heat, cover, and simmer for 3 to 4 minutes or until tender crisp. Drain in a colander and run under cold water. Drain well on paper towels.

2. Alternately thread the potatoes, chicken, and green onions (folded in half) onto eight (12-inch) skewers. Coat chicken and vegetables with nonstick cooking spray and season with salt and pepper.

3. Heat a grill or grill pan to medium-high heat and coat with nonstick cooking spray. Cook skewers 14 to 16 minutes or until chicken is no longer pink in center, turning occasionally.

4. Meanwhile, combine the fruit spread, pineapple and reserved juice, and horseradish in a small bowl. Serve sauce alongside skewers.

 Cook's Note

It's important to run cold water over the potatoes as soon as they are drained. Otherwise they will continue to cook as they cool and won't hold together.

Grilled Chicken & Kale Salad with Orange

Between the dark green kale and the bright orange segments, this salad pops with color. There's no need to toss, just let the dressing lightly coat the ingredients so the flavors stay "on top"!

SERVES 4

 4 (4-ounce) boneless, skinless chicken
   breasts, flattened to an even thickness
   Salt and freshly ground black pepper
 1 (5-ounce) package baby kale mix
 2 cups orange sections
   (about 4 navel oranges)
 3 tablespoons balsamic vinegar
 3 tablespoons canola oil
 2 tablespoons honey
 ½ teaspoon chopped fresh rosemary, optional

1. Heat a grill or grill pan to medium-high heat.

2. Coat both sides of the chicken with nonstick cooking spray and season with salt and pepper. Cook chicken 4 to 6 minutes on each side or until no longer pink in center. Place on cutting board to cool before chopping.

3. Place kale mix on a platter or large bowl and top with the orange segments and chicken.

4. In a small bowl, whisk together the vinegar, oil, and honey. Spoon over the salad and season with salt and pepper. Sprinkle with the rosemary, if desired.

 Cook's Note

If you don't have fresh rosemary, you can use the same amount of the dried variety. This is about the only herb where you can use the same amount of fresh or dried!

PER SERVING
Calories: 320
Fat: 14 g
Saturated fat: 1.5 g
Cholesterol: 65 mg
Sodium: 100 mg
Carbohydrate: 24 g
Dietary fiber: 3 g
Sugars: 19 g
Protein: 26 g

Smashed Avocado & Turkey Burger

The next time you plan on throwing burgers on the grill, rethink your menu and serve these instead. Imagine biting into a burger slathered with a mixture of avocado, jalapeño, and a splash of lemon and served on a grilled bun with arugula (and possibly a sweet red onion slice). These are great cooked on a grill pan, too!

SERVES 4

- 1 pound lean ground turkey
  Salt and freshly ground black pepper
- 1 avocado, peeled and pitted
- 1 jalapeño pepper, seeded (if desired) and minced
- 2 tablespoons freshly squeezed lemon juice
- 4 whole wheat or onion rolls
- 2 cups arugula
- 4 thin slices red onion, optional

1. Shape turkey into four ½-inch-thick patties. Season with salt and pepper.

2. Heat a grill or grill pan to medium-high heat. Coat grill rack with cooking spray and cook the patties 5 to 6 minutes on each side or until no longer pink in center.

3. Meanwhile, roughly mash the avocado with jalapeño and lemon juice. Season with salt and pepper.

4. Coat cut side of the rolls with nonstick cooking spray and grill 30 to 45 seconds on each side or until grill marks appear.

5. Place the arugula on the bottom half of each roll. Top with onion slices, if desired, turkey patties, and the avocado mixture. Top with remaining bun halves and press down gently to adhere.

PER SERVING
Calories: 360
Fat: 16 g
Saturated fat: 3.5 g
Cholesterol: 85 mg
Sodium: 310 mg
Carbohydrate: 27 g
Dietary fiber: 6 g
Sugars: 5 g
Protein: 27 g

 Cook's Note
You can purchase premade lean ground turkey patties in major supermarkets.

Jerked Chicken, Pineapple, & Red Peppers

If you've never grilled fruit, you're in for an easy treat! The grilling brings out the natural sweetness of the fruit and caramelizes it slightly. Try peaches, nectarines...even mango! It's delicious hot off the grill, at room temperature, or even chilled. It's even great for dessert. For a milder dish, use one tablespoon of the jerk seasoning. If you like a bit more heat, go for the full two tablespoons.

SERVES 4

- 4 (4-ounce) boneless, skinless chicken breasts, flattened to an even thickness
- 1–2 tablespoons jerk seasoning
- 1 fresh pineapple, peeled and cored
- 1 red bell pepper, cut into ½-inch-thick rings
  Salt and freshly ground black pepper
- 2 limes, divided use
- 4 teaspoons extra virgin olive oil

PER SERVING

Calories: 230

Fat: 8 g

Saturated fat: 1.5 g

Cholesterol: 65 mg

Sodium: 270 mg

Carbohydrate: 16 g

Dietary fiber: 2 g

Sugars: 12 g

Protein: 24 g

1. Sprinkle both sides of the chicken with the jerk seasoning. Let stand 10 minutes.

2. Meanwhile, heat a grill or grill pan to medium-high heat.

3. Cut the pineapple in half lengthwise and cut into eight wedges. Coat the pineapple wedges and bell pepper with cooking spray.

4. Grill pineapple and bell pepper for 12 to 14 minutes or until tender, turning occasionally.

5. Place pineapple on serving platter. Chop the peppers and season with salt and pepper.

6. Coat both sides of the chicken with cooking spray. Cook 4 minutes on each side or until no longer pink in center. Place chicken on platter and top with the peppers. Squeeze the juice of 1 lime evenly over all and spoon the oil evenly over the peppers. Cut the remaining lime into four wedges and serve alongside.

 Cook's Note

To save time, look for peeled and cored pineapple in the produce section of most major supermarkets.

Chili in a Hurry

Want chili, but don't want to wait? This chili tastes as though it's been cooking on the back burner all day long, with deep flavors of green chilies and a heady aroma of cumin in every bite!

SERVES 4

1	pound lean ground turkey
4	poblano peppers (or 2 green bell peppers), seeded and chopped, divided use
1	(14.5-ounce) can diced tomatoes with chili seasonings
1	(15-ounce) can kidney beans, rinsed and drained
3	cups water
1½	teaspoons ground cumin, or to taste
¼	cup ketchup
	Salt and freshly ground black pepper

1. Heat a large saucepan over medium-high heat. Add turkey and all but ¼ cup of the peppers. Cook 4 minutes, or until turkey is browned, stirring frequently and breaking up the larger pieces as it cooks. Add the tomatoes, beans, water, and cumin and bring to a boil. Reduce heat and simmer, uncovered, for 20 minutes, or until thickened slightly.

2. Remove from heat and stir in the ketchup. Let stand 10 minutes to allow flavors to develop; season with salt and pepper. Serve topped with the remaining ¼ cup of peppers.

 Cook's Note When working with chili peppers, if you're not wearing gloves, it's important to wash and dry your hands thoroughly before and after handling them to prevent skin irritation.

PER SERVING
Calories: 340
Fat: 9 g
Saturated fat: 2.5 g
Cholesterol: 85 mg
Sodium: 690 mg
Carbohydrate: 33 g
Dietary fiber: 7 g
Sugars: 8 g
Protein: 30 g

Chicken Kalamata Salad

Instead of a typical salad of "greens and things," why not change it up and put everything on top of the greens for a completely different taste. The color, the shine, and the freshness of this salad will make you look forward to making it again and again!

SERVES 4

2 cups chopped cooked chicken breast

1 ½ cups grape tomatoes, halved

16 pitted Kalamata olives, coarsely chopped

⅓ cup chopped fresh basil

3 tablespoons extra virgin olive oil

1 garlic clove, minced, optional

4 cups arugula

1. Combine all ingredients except arugula in a large bowl. Toss gently until well blended. Serve over the arugula.

 For a variation, serve the chicken mixture on long leaves of romaine and eat it as you would a hot dog!

PER SERVING

Calories: 260

Fat: 17 g

Saturated fat: 2 g

Cholesterol: 60 mg

Sodium: 320 mg

Carbohydrate: 4 g

Dietary fiber: 2 g

Sugars: 2 g

Protein: 23 g

Turkey, Raisin, & Allspice Stuffed Peppers

Traditionally, stuffed peppers meant heating the oven and then baking for an hour. This skillet version is ready in a fraction of the time and captures all of the characteristics and textures of the longer version.

SERVES 4

¼	cup chopped pecans
1	pound lean ground turkey
1½	teaspoons ground allspice or cinnamon, divided use
1	(8-ounce) can tomato sauce
½	cup raisins
¼	cup water
2	green or red bell peppers, halved lengthwise, stems and seeds removed

1. Heat a large nonstick skillet over medium-high heat. Add the pecans and cook 2 minutes or until beginning to brown lightly, stirring frequently. Set aside on separate plate.

2. Add the turkey and 1 teaspoon of the allspice to the skillet and cook until browned. Reduce heat to medium-low and stir in the tomato sauce, raisins, and water. Place the pepper halves, cut side down, on top of the turkey mixture and press down gently. Cover and cook 20 minutes or until the peppers are tender.

3. Place the peppers on four dinner plates. Stir the remaining ½ teaspoon allspice into the turkey mixture and season with salt and pepper. Spoon the turkey mixture into pepper halves and sprinkle with pecans.

PER SERVING

Calories: 310

Fat: 14 g

Saturated fat: 3 g

Cholesterol: 85 mg

Sodium: 360 mg

Carbohydrate: 22 g

Dietary fiber: 4 g

Sugars: 15 g

Protein: 24 g

Cook's Note

Toasting the pecans enhances their nutty flavor. It's important to remove them from the skillet right away or they will continue to cook and possibly burn.

Tarragon-Dijon Chicken & Green Pea Orzo

Dijon mustard and tarragon have always been a perfect match, but when paired with chicken and browned in a skillet, they transform into a rich, deep brown sauce that is perfect for dipping!

SERVES 4

- 3 ounces orzo pasta
- 1 cup frozen green peas
- 3 tablespoons extra virgin olive oil, divided use
- 2 tablespoons Dijon mustard
- ½ teaspoon dried tarragon
- 4 (4-ounce) boneless, skinless chicken breasts, flattened to an even thickness
  Salt and freshly ground black pepper
- ¼ cup water

PER SERVING

Calories: 330

Fat: 14 g

Saturated fat: 2.5 g

Cholesterol: 65 mg

Sodium: 260 mg

Carbohydrate: 21 g

Dietary fiber: 3 g

Sugars: 3 g

Protein: 28 g

1. Cook orzo according to package directions, adding green peas 2 minutes before end of cooking time.

2. Meanwhile, whisk together 2 tablespoons of the oil with the mustard and tarragon in a small bowl. Reserve 2 tablespoons of the mixture and set aside. Brush both sides of the chicken with the remaining mustard mixture and season with salt and pepper.

3. Heat a large nonstick skillet over medium heat. Cook the chicken 5 to 6 minutes on each side or until no longer pink in center.

4. Drain pasta mixture and toss with the remaining 1 tablespoon of oil. Season with salt and pepper. Place on a serving platter and top with the chicken.

5. To pan residue, whisk in the water and bring to a boil over medium heat. Boil 45 to 60 seconds or until reduced to 2 tablespoons. Remove from the heat and whisk in the reserved mustard mixture until well blended. Spoon alongside chicken for dipping.

 Cook's Note

Since chicken breasts come in a variety of sizes and vary in thickness, flattening the thicker part with a meat mallet or the bottom of a can will provide better results and even cooking.

Simmered Chicken in Sweet Peppers & Tomatoes

In this cool weather staple, fall-apart tender chicken, simmered in a mixture of herbed tomato sauce, mushrooms, and tons of sweet peppers, is spooned over hot egg noodles. It's comfort redefined!

SERVES 4

- 4 (4-ounce) boneless, skinless chicken thighs, trimmed of fat
- 1 (8-ounce) package sliced mushrooms
- 1 (14-ounce) package frozen peppers and onions
- 1 (8-ounce) can tomato sauce with basil, garlic, and oregano
- 6 ounces no-yolk egg noodles
- ½ cup water
- 3 tablespoons ketchup

1. Heat a large nonstick skillet over medium-high heat. Coat both sides of chicken with cooking spray and cook 4 minutes on each side or until browned. Add the mushrooms, peppers and onions, and tomato sauce and bring to a boil. Reduce heat, cover, and simmer 40 minutes or until chicken is no longer pink in center.

2. Cook the noodles according to package directions.

3. Meanwhile, combine the water and ketchup in a small bowl until well blended. Remove the chicken from the heat and gently stir in the ketchup mixture. Season with salt and pepper, cover, and let stand 10 minutes to absorb flavors. Serve over drained noodles.

PER SERVING
Calories: 370
Fat: 8 g
Saturated fat: 2 g
Cholesterol: 100 mg
Sodium: 560 mg
Carbohydrate: 45 g
Dietary fiber: 5 g
Sugars: 10 g
Protein: 27 g

Cook's Note

Ketchup acts as a multitasker (not as a condiment) here, because the sugar and vinegar in the ketchup help to lift the flavors of the other ingredients. It also adds a small amount of sweetness, tartness, and tomato flavor.

Basil-Baked Chicken & Potatoes

It's refreshing to incorporate a variety of cheeses into your menu planning. By choosing stronger-flavored varieties and using smaller amounts, the robust cheese flavors can be stretched without going overboard. Look for sharp provolone in your grocer's deli and ask them to slice the cheese for you.

SERVES 4

- 4 (4-ounce) boneless, skinless chicken breasts, flattened to an even thickness
  Salt and freshly ground black pepper
- 8 whole fresh basil leaves
- 4 deli slices sharp provolone cheese (about 3 ounces)
- 2 plum tomatoes, cut into 4 slices each
- 1 pound small new potatoes, quartered, or fingerling potatoes, halved lengthwise
- 2 teaspoons extra virgin olive oil

1. Heat oven to 425 degrees.

2. Coat both sides of the chicken with cooking spray, season with salt and pepper, and place on a foil-lined baking sheet. Top each breast with 2 basil leaves, a cheese slice, and 2 tomato rounds and coat with cooking spray.

3. Toss the potatoes with the oil, season with salt and pepper, and arrange around the chicken.

4. Bake 22 to 25 minutes or until chicken is no longer pink in center and potatoes are tender.

 Cook's Note For a variation, substitute three-quarters' cup shredded Italian-blend cheese with garlic for the provolone.

PER SERVING
Calories: 310
Fat: 11 g
Saturated fat: 5 g
Cholesterol: 85 mg
Sodium: 250 mg
Carbohydrate: 20 g
Dietary fiber: 3 g
Sugars: 2 g
Protein: 31 g

Seafood

Grilled Shrimp & Veggies with Balsamic Reduction

Balsamic vinegar has a powerful flavor, but when it's reduced, it takes on sweet, concentrated characteristics. The result is more like a tangy sweet sauce than a pungent vinegar. A little spoonful goes a long way, too!

SERVES 4

- 2 zucchini, cut in half lengthwise
- 1 red onion, cut into ½-inch-thick slices
- ½ cup balsamic vinegar
- 1 pound peeled raw medium shrimp
- 1 pint grape tomatoes, halved
- ¼ cup chopped fresh parsley
  Salt and freshly ground black pepper

1. Heat a grill or grill pan to medium-high heat. Coat the grill rack and both sides of the zucchini and onion with cooking spray. Cook 8 minutes.

2. Meanwhile, bring the vinegar to a boil over high heat in a small saucepan. Boil for 3 minutes or until reduced to ¼ cup liquid. Set aside to cool and thicken slightly.

3. Coat the shrimp with cooking spray. Turn the zucchini and onions and add the shrimp to the grill. Cook the shrimp and vegetables 5 minutes or until shrimp are opaque in center, turning occasionally.

4. Coarsely chop the zucchini and onion and place in a large bowl with the tomatoes and parsley. Toss gently to combine. Place shrimp on top of the vegetables. Drizzle vinegar evenly over all. Season with salt and pepper. Do not toss.

 Cook's Note The shrimp can be replaced with chicken tenderloins, if desired. Small chicken tenderloins and medium shrimp will cook in about the same amount of time.

PER SERVING
Calories: 180
Fat: 1.5 g
Saturated fat: 0 g
Cholesterol: 190 mg
Sodium: 135 mg
Carbohydrate: 15 g
Dietary fiber: 3 g
Sugars: 11 g
Protein: 26 g

Tilapia & Black Bean Bowls

Bring out the spoons! Pan-seared tender fillets of tilapia are served on a brothy bed of black beans, fresh tomatoes, and green chilies, then topped with avocado and a generous squeeze of lime. Be sure to serve this in shallow soup bowls to contain the flavorful juices!

SERVES 4

- 4 (4- to 6-ounce) tilapia fillets or other lean white fish, such as snapper or flounder, rinsed and patted dry
- Salt and freshly ground black pepper
- 1 (15-ounce) can black beans, rinsed and drained
- 1 cup chopped fresh tomatoes
- ¼ cup water
- 1 (4-ounce) can chopped mild green chilies
- 1 lime, cut in half
- 1 avocado, pitted and chopped

1. Heat a large nonstick skillet over medium heat. Coat both sides of the fish fillets with cooking spray and season with pepper. Cook 3 minutes on each side or until it flakes easily with a fork.

2. Meanwhile, combine the beans, tomatoes, and water in a medium saucepan and bring to a boil. Reduce heat, cover, and cook 2 to 3 minutes or until heated through. Stir in the chilies and season with salt and pepper.

3. Divide the bean mixture evenly between four shallow soup bowls. Top with the fish, squeeze the juice of half a lime over all, and top with avocado. Season with salt and pepper. Cut remaining lime half into four wedges and serve alongside.

Cook's Note For a spicier dish, use hot green chilies.

PER SERVING

Calories: 270
Fat: 8 g
Saturated fat: 1.5 g
Cholesterol: 50 mg
Sodium: 240 mg
Carbohydrate: 22 g
Dietary fiber: 9 g
Sugars: 4 g
Protein: 29 g

Snapper on White Beans with Tomatoes & Green Olives

The cooking of this fast-paced dish goes so quickly that you definitely need to have everything prepped (cans opened, ingredients chopped and measured out) before you start! Then pull up a chair, sit down, and savor every bite!

SERVES 4

- 1 (15-ounce) can navy beans, rinsed and drained
- 4 (4- to 6-ounce) snapper fillets or other lean white fish, such as tilapia or flounder, rinsed and patted dry
  Salt and freshly ground black pepper
- 1 (14.5-ounce) can diced fire-roasted tomatoes with garlic
- 12 small pimento-stuffed green olives, coarsely chopped
- ½ teaspoon fresh or dried rosemary, chopped, optional
- ¼ cup chopped fresh parsley
- ½ cup crumbled feta cheese

PER SERVING
Calories: 270
Fat: 7 g
Saturated fat: 2.5 g
Cholesterol: 50 mg
Sodium: 720 mg
Carbohydrate: 22 g
Dietary fiber: 8 g
Sugars: 3 g
Protein: 32 g

1. Divide the beans equally between four shallow soup bowls.

2. Coat both sides of fish fillets with nonstick cooking spray; season with salt and pepper. Heat a large nonstick skillet over medium-high heat. Cook fish 3 minutes on each side or until it flakes easily with a fork. Place on top of the beans.

3. Combine the tomatoes, olives, and rosemary, if desired, in the skillet. Bring to a boil over medium-high heat and cook for 1 minute. Remove from heat. Spoon over the fish and sprinkle with parsley and feta.

Cook's Note

The heat from the fish and the tomato mixture will heat the beans just enough.

Grilled Tuna Salad on Butter Lettuce

Plan on sitting down to this fresh, fast salad in a matter of minutes! Sometimes super simple is best, and this recipe is it. Fresh tuna is quickly grilled and served over tender butter lettuce with a tangy, sweet balsamic vinaigrette. So pretty, so fast, and so good!

SERVES 4

4	(4-ounce) tuna steaks (about ¾-inch thick), rinsed and patted dry
	Salt and freshly ground black pepper
3	tablespoons canola oil
2	tablespoons honey
1½	tablespoons balsamic vinegar
1½	tablespoons Worcestershire sauce
6	cups butter lettuce (or kale mix)
½	cup chopped red onion, optional

1. Heat grill or grill pan to medium-high heat. Coat the grill rack and both sides of the tuna steaks with nonstick cooking spray and season with salt and pepper. Cook 2 minutes on each side or to desired doneness. Place on cutting board.

2. Whisk together the oil, honey, vinegar, and Worcestershire sauce in a small bowl.

3. Place the lettuce on a platter or in a large salad bowl. Cut tuna in ¼-inch-thick slices against the grain, place on the lettuce, and sprinkle with onions, if desired. Drizzle the dressing evenly over all and season with salt and pepper.

Cook's Note Unlike other fish, fresh tuna is best served rare or medium-rare and very pink in the center. Do not overcook or it will be tough.

PER SERVING

Calories: 320

Fat: 17 g

Saturated fat: 2.5 g

Cholesterol: 45 mg

Sodium: 115 mg

Carbohydrate: 13 g

Dietary fiber: 1 g

Sugars: 11 g

Protein: 29 g

Grilled Lemon Fish with Sun-Dried Tomato Bulgur

This dish of fish and bulgur is built with "layers" of flavors. Grilled grouper is topped with freshly squeezed lemon juice, extra virgin olive oil, and dill, and served with bulgur tossed with a sun-dried tomato pesto!

SERVES 4

1   cup bulgur
4   (4- to 6-ounce) grouper or other firm
        white fish fillets, such as cod or mahi
        mahi, rinsed and patted dry
      Salt and freshly ground black pepper
½   cup sun-dried tomato pesto
      Zest and juice from 1 large lemon
1   tablespoon extra virgin olive oil
4   teaspoons dried dill

1. Cook bulgur according to package directions.

2. Meanwhile, heat a grill or grill pan to medium-high heat. Coat grill rack and both sides of the fish with nonstick cooking spray and season with salt and pepper. Cook 4 to 5 minutes on each side or until fish flakes easily with a fork.

3. Using a fork, fluff the bulgur and stir in the pesto and lemon zest.

4. Serve the bulgur mixture alongside the fish. Spoon the lemon juice over the fish, drizzle with the oil, and sprinkle with dill. Season with salt and pepper.

Cook's Note

A microplane (a handheld narrow grater) is a handy and inexpensive tool for zesting citrus fruit or grating fresh ginger or garlic, and it's easy to clean as well.

PER SERVING
Calories: 330
Fat: 9 g
Saturated fat: 1.5 g
Cholesterol: 45 mg
Sodium: 370 mg
Carbohydrate: 36 g
Dietary fiber: 8 g
Sugars: 3 g
Protein: 28 g

Tilapia & Vegetable Packets with Rosemary-Mustard Sauce

Foil packets are not only fun to make, they're fun to serve. They also serve a serious purpose, capturing the juices while cooking so the ingredients are kept moist and tender. This is particularly helpful when cooking delicate pieces of fish and vegetables. In these little packets, asparagus and green peas are cooked with tilapia fillets then served with a light sauce of olive oil, mustard, and rosemary.

SERVES 4

8	ounces asparagus spears, ends trimmed, cut into 2-inch pieces
1 ⅓	cups frozen green peas, thawed
4	(4- to 6-ounce) tilapia fillets, or other lean white fish, such as snapper or flounder, rinsed and patted dry
3	tablespoons extra virgin olive oil, divided use
	Salt and freshly ground black pepper
	Paprika, optional
2	tablespoons Dijon mustard
1	tablespoon water
½	teaspoon chopped fresh or dried rosemary or Italian seasoning

PER SERVING

Calories: 250

Fat: 13 g

Saturated fat: 2 g

Cholesterol: 55 mg

Sodium: 290 mg

Carbohydrate: 9 g

Dietary fiber: 3 g

Sugars: 3 g

Protein: 26 g

1. Preheat broiler and place oven rack about 5 to 6 inches from heat source. Tear off four (12-inch-square) pieces of foil.

2. Divide equal amounts of the asparagus and peas on the foil sheets. Top with the fish fillets. Spoon 2 tablespoons of the oil evenly over all; season with salt and pepper and sprinkle with paprika, if desired. Bring the short ends of the foil together and fold twice to seal; fold in the sides to seal, leaving room for steam.

3. Place under broiler and broil 10 minutes or until fish flakes easily with a fork.

4. Meanwhile, whisk together the mustard, water, and rosemary in a small bowl. Slowly whisk in the remaining 1 tablespoon of oil until well blended. Unwrap each packet and drizzle the sauce evenly over each serving. Sprinkle with additional black pepper before serving.

 Cook's Note

For a fancier presentation, you can use parchment paper instead of foil.

Ginger-Lime Grilled Salmon with Mango Skewers

Serve this the next time you want rave reviews. It's gorgeous, packed with sweet-hot flavor, and has the added bonus of being super easy...and super fast! You'll need eight (eight-inch) skewers. If using wooden skewers, soak them for ten to thirty minutes in warm water before threading to keep them from burning.

SERVES 4

- 4   (4- to 6-ounce) salmon fillets, rinsed and patted dry
- 2   tablespoons jerk seasoning
- 2   cups ripe but firm mango chunks, cut in 1-inch cubes
- 2   tablespoons sugar
- 2   tablespoons lime juice
- 2   teaspoons grated ginger
      Freshly ground black pepper
- ¼   cup chopped fresh mint or cilantro, optional

PER SERVING

Calories: 280
Fat: 9 g
Saturated fat: 2 g
Cholesterol: 60 mg
Sodium: 490 mg
Carbohydrate: 26 g
Dietary fiber: 1 g
Sugars: 23 g
Protein: 22 g

1. Heat a grill or grill pan to medium-high heat. Coat grill rack and both sides of the salmon with nonstick cooking spray and sprinkle the flesh side evenly with the jerk seasoning, pressing down lightly to adhere. Grill salmon (skin side up) for 5 minutes.

2. Meanwhile, thread ½ cup of the mango using two skewers side by side, to prevent the mango from slipping and sliding on the skewers. Repeat with the remaining mango and two more skewers and coat with nonstick cooking spray.

3. Turn the salmon carefully and place the mango skewers on grill alongside it. Cook for 5 to 6 minutes, or until salmon is just opaque in center, gently turning skewers occasionally.

4. Combine the sugar, lime juice, and ginger in a small bowl and stir until sugar dissolves.

5. Serve mango alongside the salmon, spooning the lime mixture over the salmon. Sprinkle with black pepper and mint, if desired.

 Cook's Note You can also use frozen mango cubes that are partially thawed—simply let stand ten minutes at room temperature.

Fish with Chimichurri-Style Sauce & Grilled Corn

Fresh corn on the cob tastes so good, whether you broil in or grill out. It's an earthy treat to serve alongside fish, especially with this citrusy chimichurri-style sauce. Chimichurri, which hails from Argentina, is traditionally made with parsley, garlic, vinegar, and chilies, but you can vary it by using cilantro instead of parsley, lemon juice instead of vinegar, and even by chopping the herbs differently. Either way, the end result will be delicious!

SERVES 4

- 4 ears of corn, husks and silks removed
- 4 (4- to 6-ounce) cod or other firm white fish fillets, such as grouper or mahi mahi, rinsed and patted dry
- Salt and freshly ground black pepper
- ½ cup chopped fresh parsley
- 2 tablespoons extra virgin olive oil
- 2 teaspoons lemon zest
- 1½ tablespoons lemon juice
- 1 garlic clove, minced

PER SERVING

Calories: 260
Fat: 10 g
Saturated fat: 1.5 g
Cholesterol: 50 mg
Sodium: 75 mg
Carbohydrate: 23 g
Dietary fiber: 3 g
Sugars: 5 g
Protein: 24 g

1. Preheat broiler and set oven rack 5 to 6 inches from heat source.

2. Coat ears of corn with nonstick cooking spray and place on a foil-lined baking sheet. Broil for 12 to 14 minutes, or until beginning to brown, turning occasionally. Set aside on separate plate; cover to keep warm.

3. Coat both sides of the fish fillets with nonstick cooking spray; season with pepper. Place on the baking sheet. Broil 3 minutes on each side or until fish flakes easily with a fork.

4. Meanwhile, combine the remaining ingredients in a small bowl; season with salt and pepper and set aside.

5. Spoon equal amounts of the parsley mixture on each fish fillet. Serve with the corn.

 Cook's Note: The fish and corn can be grilled over medium-high heat with the same cooking times, if desired.

Salmon with Soy Citrus

The combination of orange, soy sauce, and honey is delicious on many things, but when added to salmon and cooked under high heat, the outcome is a colorful, deep golden glaze! Adding a touch of heat at the end adds to the "mouth-explosion" of flavors. Try it, you'll see!

SERVES 4

Zest and juice of 1 navel orange
3 tablespoons light soy sauce
2 tablespoons honey
1 tablespoon white balsamic vinegar or
   balsamic vinegar
4 (4- to 6-ounce) salmon fillets, rinsed and
   patted dry
1 (8-ounce) package fresh sugar snap peas,
   trimmed
1 jalapeño pepper, minced, optional

1. Preheat broiler.

2. In a small bowl, whisk together the orange juice and zest, soy sauce, honey, and vinegar.

3. Place the salmon skin side down on a foil-lined baking sheet coated with nonstick cooking spray. Brush 1 tablespoon of the orange juice mixture evenly over the fish. Broil 7 to 8 minutes or until just opaque in center.

4. Meanwhile, heat a large nonstick skillet over medium-high heat. Coat sugar snap peas with cooking spray and cook for 3 minutes, or until just beginning to brown, stirring frequently. Set aside.

5. Add the remaining orange juice mixture to the skillet; bring to a boil over medium-high heat and boil for 2 minutes, or until reduced to 1/4 cup.

6. Drizzle the orange juice mixture over the salmon and top with minced jalapeño, if desired. Serve with the snap peas.

PER SERVING
Calories: 260
Fat: 9 g
Saturated fat: 2 g
Cholesterol: 60 mg
Sodium: 490 mg
Carbohydrate: 18 g
Dietary fiber: 2 g
Sugars: 14 g
Protein: 25 g

Cook's Note Coating the baking sheet with foil makes for super-speedy cleanup.

Green Pepper, Pineapple, & Shrimp Stir-Fry

Rice vermicelli noodles are sometimes referred to as "rice sticks." They're easy to prepare and even more fun to eat. Just let them stand in very hot water for a few minutes and they're ready. They're a nice change from rice or pasta and a good source of fiber, too!

SERVES 4

6	cups plus ⅓ cup water, divided use
1	(6-ounce) package rice vermicelli noodles
10	ounces raw, peeled shrimp
1	green bell pepper, thinly sliced
2	cups pineapple chunks, fresh or frozen and thawed
⅓	cup water
2	limes, divided use
1½	tablespoons Thai roasted red chili paste
	Salt and freshly ground black pepper

1. Bring 6 cups of the water to boil in a large saucepan over high heat. Remove from heat. Stir noodles into the water, cover, and let stand 3 minutes or until just tender. Drain and set aside in colander.

2. Heat a large nonstick skillet over medium-high heat and coat with nonstick cooking spray. Cook the shrimp for 4 minutes or until opaque, stirring occasionally. Set aside.

3. Add the bell pepper and cook for 3 minutes or until just beginning to brown. Add the pineapple and cook for 1 minute.

4. Whisk together the remaining ⅓ cup water, the juice of 1 lime, and the chili paste in a small bowl. Add to the skillet along with the shrimp and cook for 1 minute to heat through, stirring frequently.

5. Run noodles under hot water and drain well. Place in a large bowl. Top with the shrimp mixture and season with salt and pepper. Cut remaining lime into four wedges and serve alongside.

PER SERVING

Calories: 300

Fat: 2 g

Saturated fat: 0 g

Cholesterol: 120 mg

Sodium: 150 mg

Carbohydrate: 53 g

Dietary fiber: 3 g

Sugars: 10 g

Protein: 19 g

 Cook's Note The rice noodles will stick together, so rinsing them quickly in hot water will reheat and "unstick" them.

Fish with Hot Poppin' Tomatoes

Sweet grape tomatoes have become so popular and for good reason. Their concentrated sweetness lasts all year long. In this recipe, they're roasted until they burst, and their juiciness helps create a delicious sauce!

SERVES 4

1 green bell pepper, chopped
1 pint grape tomatoes
1 cup fresh or frozen cut okra, thawed, rinsed, and patted dry
4 (4- to 6-ounce) cod or other firm white fish fillets, such as grouper or mahi mahi, rinsed and patted dry
Salt and freshly ground black pepper
2 tablespoons extra virgin olive oil
1 tablespoon hot pepper sauce, or to taste
¼ cup chopped fresh parsley, optional

1. Preheat oven to 450 degrees.

2. Place the bell pepper, tomatoes, and okra on a foil-lined baking sheet. Coat vegetables with nonstick cooking spray and toss until well coated. Place vegetables in a single layer on the baking sheet. Bake 5 minutes.

3. Gently push the vegetables to one side of the baking sheet. Coat the fish fillets with cooking spray and place on the other end of the baking sheet. Season with salt and pepper.

4. Bake 12 to 15 minutes or until fish flakes easily with a fork and tomatoes begin to split or "pop."

5. Meanwhile, whisk together the oil and hot pepper sauce until well blended and set aside.

6. Serve the fish topped with the vegetables and drizzle evenly with the oil mixture. Season with salt and pepper. Sprinkle with parsley, if desired.

PER SERVING
Calories: 190
Fat: 8 g
Saturated fat: 1 g
Cholesterol: 50 mg
Sodium: 100 mg
Carbohydrate: 7 g
Dietary fiber: 2 g
Sugars: 4 g
Protein: 22 g

Cook's Note

To thaw frozen vegetables quickly, place in a colander and run under cold water briefly. Drain well.

Spiced Thai Soup with Shrimp & Mushrooms

Roasted red chili paste is a staple in Thai cooking. A concentrated blend of red chilies and Thai spices, such as lemongrass, cilantro, garlic, and kaffir lime, it can be used as a stir-fry seasoning, a soup base, or as a spicy condiment for chicken. Add a small amount at a time to regulate the flavor AND the heat level. For a mild soup, one tablespoon should do it; if you'd like it spicier, use two tablespoons.

SERVES 4

1 (8-ounce) package sliced mushrooms
1 (14.5-ounce) can diced tomatoes or fire-roasted diced tomatoes with garlic
½ cup water
1-2 tablespoons Thai roasted red chili paste
10 ounces raw, peeled shrimp
1 cup light coconut milk
½ cup chopped fresh cilantro, divided use
1 tablespoon sugar, optional
Salt and freshly ground black pepper

1. Over medium-high heat, coat a large saucepan with nonstick cooking spray. Add the mushrooms and cook 4 minutes or until tender. Add the tomatoes, water, and chili paste. Bring to a boil, then reduce heat, cover, and simmer 10 minutes. Add the shrimp. Cover and cook 5 minutes, or until opaque in center.

2. Remove from heat and stir in coconut milk, ¼ cup of the cilantro, and sugar, if desired. Cover and let stand 5 minutes to absorb flavors. Season with salt and pepper. Spoon into four soup bowls and top with the remaining cilantro.

Cook's Note

You can find roasted red chili paste in the international section of major supermarkets. Be sure to read the label closely; you don't want to confuse red chili paste with red curry paste.

PER SERVING

Calories: 130
Fat: 4.5 g
Saturated fat: 3 g
Cholesterol: 85 mg
Sodium: 250 mg
Carbohydrate: 9 g
Dietary fiber: 2 g
Sugars: 5 g
Protein: 15 g

Greek Grouper Wraps

Pick your fish of choice for this recipe, but choose a firm variety. Firmer fish are easier to manage on the grill and don't fall apart when turning. The milky white fish contrasts with the grill marks and makes for a mouthwatering sight!

SERVES 4

- 4 (8-inch) whole wheat or flour tortillas
- 4 (4- to 6-ounce) grouper or other firm white fish fillets, such as cod or mahi mahi, rinsed and patted dry
- Salt and freshly ground black pepper
- 1 cup 2 percent plain Greek yogurt
- 1 tablespoon dried dill
- 2 garlic cloves, minced
- 3 tablespoons water
- 4 cups shredded romaine or baby kale mix
- 1 lemon, quartered, optional

1. Preheat grill or grill pan to medium-high heat.

2. Coat both sides of the tortillas with cooking spray and grill 30 seconds on each side or until grill marks appear. Set aside and cover to keep warm.

3. Coat the grill and both sides of the fish with cooking spray. Lightly season with salt and pepper. Cook 4 to 5 minutes on each side or until fish flakes easily with a fork. Break into smaller pieces.

4. Meanwhile, stir together the yogurt, dill, garlic, and water in a small bowl. Add salt and pepper to taste.

5. Top each tortilla with equal amounts of the romaine, spoon yogurt mixture down the center, and top with the flaked fish. Serve with lemon wedges, if desired.

PER SERVING

Calories: 330

Fat: 8 g

Saturated fat: 3.5 g

Cholesterol: 45 mg

Sodium: 340 mg

Carbohydrate: 29 g

Dietary fiber: 6 g

Sugars: 4 g

Protein: 34 g

Cook's Note

Be sure to pat the fish dry before coating with cooking spray. This ensures proper browning.

Grilled Mahi-Mahi & Broccoli with Red Pepper-Tomato Salad

In this easy "dinner on the grill," the vegetables, fish, and even the toppings are all tossed on the grill (or grill pan) at various stages. Tossing the grilled peppers with fresh tomatoes, herbs, and a splash of balsamic vinegar makes for a super-easy and flavorful topping.

SERVES 4

- 1 pound broccoli, cut into 8 spears
- 1 large red bell pepper, halved lengthwise and seeded
  Salt and freshly ground black pepper
- 4 (4- to 6-ounce) mahi mahi or other firm white fish fillets, such as grouper or cod, rinsed and patted dry
- 1 cup chopped fresh tomatoes
- 2 tablespoons chopped fresh basil or parsley
- 1 tablespoon balsamic vinegar

1. Heat a grill or grill pan to medium heat. Liberally coat broccoli, peppers, and grill rack with nonstick cooking spray and season with salt and pepper. Cook 15 minutes or until broccoli is tender and lightly charred, turning occasionally.

2. Place broccoli on separate plate and cover to keep warm. Place peppers on cutting board and cool slightly before chopping.

3. Meanwhile, coat both sides of the fish with nonstick cooking spray and season with salt and pepper. Grill 4 to 5 minutes on each side or until fish flakes easily with a fork.

4. Combine the chopped peppers with the tomatoes, basil, and vinegar in a medium bowl and season with salt and pepper. Top the fish with the tomato mixture and serve with the broccoli.

Cook's Note You can also reverse the serving order and serve the fish on a bed of the tomato salad rather than topping the fish.

PER SERVING

Calories: 170
Fat: 1.5 g
Saturated fat: 0 g
Cholesterol: 85 mg
Sodium: 150 mg
Carbohydrate: 13 g
Dietary fiber: 5 g
Sugars: 6 g
Protein: 26 g

Honey Mustard Cod with Pecan Topping

Naturally sweet carrots are roasted alongside fish fillets that are drizzled with a honey-soy mixture and piled with finely chopped pecans...a truly scrumptious combination!

SERVES 4

1	pound carrots, quartered lengthwise and cut into 2-inch pieces
	Salt and freshly ground black pepper
2	tablespoons honey
1 ½	tablespoons light soy sauce
2	teaspoons prepared yellow mustard
4	(4- to 6-ounce) cod or other firm white fish fillets, such as grouper or mahi mahi, rinsed and patted dry
½	cup finely chopped pecans

1. Preheat oven to 425 degrees.

2. Place the carrots on a foil-lined baking sheet. Liberally coat carrots with cooking spray and arrange in a single layer. Season with salt and pepper and bake 20 minutes.

3. Meanwhile, whisk together the honey, soy sauce, and mustard in a small bowl.

4. Move the carrots to one side of the baking sheet. Arrange the fish fillets on the baking sheet with the carrots. Spoon the honey mixture evenly over the top of the fillets and carefully mound the pecans on top. Bake 10 to 12 minutes or until fish flakes easily with a fork. Serve with the carrots, scraping any remaining nuts and sauce from the baking sheet onto the fish.

PER SERVING

Calories: 270

Fat: 12 g

Saturated fat: 1 g

Cholesterol: 50 mg

Sodium: 370 mg

Carbohydrate: 21 g

Dietary fiber: 4 g

Sugars: 14 g

Protein: 23 g

Cook's Note

Scraping the remaining nuts and sauce off the foil adds another layer of flavor. They absorb some of the sweet concentrated drippings of the honey mixture.

Vegetarian

Grilled Veggie & Goat Cheese Toasts

Simple ingredients often make the best meals. Grilled veggies are combined with fresh tomatoes and white beans and spooned over grilled slices of multigrain bread spread with goat cheese. The white beans take on the flavors of the other ingredients and add body, fiber, and protein. Every bite explodes with flavor!

SERVES 4

- 1 zucchini, cut in half lengthwise
- 1 onion, cut into ½-inch-thick rounds
- 6 ounces multigrain bakery bread, cut into 8 (½-inch-thick) slices
- 1 (4-ounce) package fresh goat cheese
- 1 cup chopped fresh tomatoes
- ½ (16-ounce) can navy beans, rinsed and drained
  Salt and freshly ground black pepper

1. Preheat grill or grill pan to medium-high heat.

2. Coat both sides of zucchini and onion with cooking spray and grill 8 minutes on each side or until just tender. Place on cutting board and chop coarsely.

3. Meanwhile, coat both sides of bread slices with cooking spray and grill 1 to 2 minutes on each side or until grill marks appear. Gently spread equal amounts of goat cheese on each bread slice.

4. Combine the zucchini, onion, tomatoes, and beans in a medium bowl. Season with salt and pepper. Spoon equal amounts over each bread slice.

Cook's Note

If the bread purchased in your grocer's bakery is not already sliced, have them slice it for you.

PER SERVING

Calories: 260
Fat: 8 g
Saturated fat: 4 g
Cholesterol: 20 mg
Sodium: 410 mg
Carbohydrate: 38 g
Dietary fiber: 6 g
Sugars: 7 g
Protein: 12 g

Fresh Spinach-Red Pepper Frittata

Frittatas can be made in a variety of ways. You don't have to flip this one…just release gently and slide onto a plate! The amount of spinach used will look massive when you first add it to the skillet, but in less than a minute, that huge mound will shrink to fit into the skillet nicely. Serve with a simple salad of melon wedges on spring greens with a splash of fresh lemon to round out the meal!

SERVES 4

1½ cups chopped onions
1½ cups chopped red bell pepper
2 eggs plus 4 egg whites
2 tablespoons water
1 teaspoon dried basil
    Salt and freshly ground black pepper
4 cups fresh baby spinach
⅓ cup shredded reduced-fat sharp cheddar
    cheese
1 plum tomato, chopped, optional

PER SERVING
Calories: 130
Fat: 5 g
Saturated fat: 2 g
Cholesterol: 100 mg
Sodium: 190 mg
Carbohydrate: 11 g
Dietary fiber: 3 g
Sugars: 6 g
Protein: 11 g

1. Heat a large nonstick skillet over medium heat. Coat onions and peppers with cooking spray and cook 6 minutes or until golden, stirring frequently.

2. Meanwhile, whisk together the eggs, egg whites, water, and basil. Season with salt and pepper.

3. Add the spinach to the onions and peppers. Using two utensils, toss 30 seconds or until spinach is slightly wilted but still holding its shape. Reduce heat to low and pour the egg mixture evenly over all. Cover and cook 10 minutes or until "puffed" and just set in the center.

4. Remove from heat, sprinkle with the cheese and tomato, if desired, and season with salt and pepper. Cover and let stand 5 minutes to allow cheese to melt.

5. To remove, gently run a silicone spatula around the outer edges, lifting gently to release the frittata from the skillet. Slide onto a dinner plate and cut into four wedges.

An easy way to stir the mound of spinach is to use two utensils, such as a fork and large spoon, and toss as you would a stir-fry.

Spinach-Provolone Baked Pasta

One-dish meals are super popular, especially freezer-friendly ones. This is a great recipe to double; eat one and pop the other in the freezer for another time. That way, you're doing half the work and making half the mess while doubling your meals!

SERVES 4

- 6 ounces whole grain spaghetti, broken into thirds, or penne
- ½ cup small curd cottage cheese
- 1½ teaspoons dried Italian seasoning
- 1¾ cups reduced-sodium marinara sauce, divided use
- 2 cups fresh baby spinach
- 4 deli slices sharp provolone cheese (about 3 ounces)

1. Preheat oven to 350 degrees.

2. Cook pasta according to package directions. Drain.

3. Meanwhile, combine cottage cheese and Italian seasoning in a small bowl.

4. Combine the drained pasta with 1 cup of the marinara sauce in a medium bowl and toss to coat. Place half the pasta in a 2-quart baking dish. Spoon teaspoons of the cottage cheese mixture evenly over the pasta. Top with spinach and remaining pasta mixture and spoon the remaining ¾ cup marinara sauce evenly over all. Cover and bake 20 minutes.

5. Top with provolone and bake, uncovered, 5 minutes or until melted.

PER SERVING

Calories: 340

Fat: 13 g

Saturated fat: 5 g

Cholesterol: 25 mg

Sodium: 550 mg

Carbohydrate: 43 g

Dietary fiber: 5 g

Sugars: 6 g

Protein: 17 g

 Cook's Note

To brown the cheese slightly, place under the broiler for one to two minutes.

Cannellini Beans & Pesto

Don't underestimate the power of grated lemon zest. Adding a little zest (the yellow skin of the lemon, not the white pith) to a dish brings out the flavor of the lemon without adding more acid or liquid. In this recipe, the lemon enhances the complex flavors of the basil pesto and brightens the whole dish.

SERVES 4

1½	cups chopped onions
1½	cups water
4	ounces pearl couscous
2	lemons, divided use
1	(15.5-ounce) can no-salt added cannellini beans, rinsed and drained
1½	cups chopped fresh tomatoes
¾	cup basil pesto
	Salt and freshly ground black pepper

1. Heat a large saucepan coated with cooking spray over medium-high heat. Add the onions and cook 4 minutes or until beginning to lightly brown on the edges, stirring frequently. Add water and couscous and bring to a boil. Reduce heat, cover, and simmer 10 minutes or until water is absorbed, stirring occasionally.

2. Meanwhile, grate 2 teaspoons lemon zest and squeeze 1 tablespoon lemon juice from one of the lemons. Cut the remaining lemon into four wedges.

3. Gently stir the beans, tomatoes, pesto, lemon zest, and lemon juice into the couscous. Cook on medium-low heat for 1 to 2 minutes to heat through. Remove from heat and season with salt and pepper. Serve with the lemon wedges.

 Cook's Note Leftovers? Add a small amount of apple cider vinegar to the chilled couscous mixture for a great pasta salad.

PER SERVING

Calories: 420

Fat: 19 g

Saturated fat: 3 g

Cholesterol: 5 mg

Sodium: 450 mg

Carbohydrate: 51 g

Dietary fiber: 9 g

Sugars: 8 g

Protein: 13 g

Quinoa-Pumpkin Seed Grain Bowls

Red tomatoes, green cilantro, black beans, and pure white goat cheese make these individual bowls pop with color, texture, and flavor!

SERVES 4

- ½ cup salted, roasted, shelled pumpkin seeds
- 1 cup quinoa
- 1 (15-ounce) can black beans, rinsed and drained
  Salt and freshly ground black pepper
- 1⅓ cups grape tomatoes, halved
- ½ cup crumbled goat cheese
- ½ cup chopped fresh cilantro

1. Heat a large saucepan over medium-high heat. Add the pumpkin seeds and cook 2 minutes or until beginning to brown lightly. Set aside on separate plate.

2. Place quinoa and black beans in the saucepan and cook according to quinoa package directions. Season with salt and pepper.

3. Divide the quinoa mixture between four bowls. Arrange the tomatoes, pumpkin seeds, and goat cheese in sections on top and sprinkle evenly with the cilantro.

Cook's Note

Sunflower seeds or a mix of pumpkin and sunflower seeds can be substituted for the pumpkin seeds, if desired.

PER SERVING

Calories: 370

Fat: 13 g

Saturated fat: 3.5 g

Cholesterol: 15 mg

Sodium: 170 mg

Carbohydrate: 48 g

Dietary fiber: 10 g

Sugars: 6 g

Protein: 19 g

Spinach-Ricotta Stuffed Portobello Caps

Dig into a savory plate of stuffed mushrooms packed with fresh spinach, ricotta cheese, and marinara sauce, topped with fresh basil and a blend of Italian cheeses. Serve a bagged salad and a few slices of crusty multigrain bread alongside to keep things simple!

SERVES 4

8   portobello mushroom caps, wiped clean with a damp cloth
2   tablespoons water
1   (5-ounce) package fresh baby spinach
½   cup part-skim ricotta cheese
⅓   cup chopped fresh basil, divided use
     Salt and freshly ground black pepper
1   cup reduced-sodium marinara sauce, divided use
¾   cup shredded Italian-blend cheese

1. Preheat oven to 425 degrees.

2. Coat both sides of the mushroom caps with cooking spray and place, stem side down, on a foil-lined baking sheet. Bake 10 minutes, turn, and bake 5 minutes or until tender.

3. Meanwhile, add water to a large skillet and place over medium-high heat. Add spinach and cook, stirring carefully, 1 to 2 minutes, or until wilted. Remove from heat and stir in the ricotta cheese and ¼ cup of the basil. Season with salt and pepper.

4. Spoon half of the marinara sauce on top of the mushroom caps (1 tablespoon per mushroom). Top with equal amounts of the spinach mixture, spoon remaining marinara sauce over all, and sprinkle with the Italian-blend cheese. Bake 10 minutes or until heated through and cheese is melted. Sprinkle with the remaining basil.

PER SERVING
Calories: 190
Fat: 11 g
Saturated fat: 5 g
Cholesterol: 25 mg
Sodium: 360 mg
Carbohydrate: 14 g
Dietary fiber: 2 g
Sugars: 6 g
Protein: 14 g

 Cook's Note When cooking the spinach, use two utensils as you would a stir-fry for easy tossing.

Feta-Artichoke Tortilla Thins

Need a quick fun meal? Toss a bagged salad with a bit of oil and vinegar to serve alongside and dinner is done! Of course, you can change out your choice of cheese and veggies, but this is a great beginning to a fun and easy meal.

SERVES 4

4   (8-inch) soft flour tortillas
½   cup no-salt-added tomato sauce
6   tablespoons crumbled feta cheese
1   ounce pine nuts or slivered almonds
½   cup finely chopped red pepper
½   cup chopped fresh basil
1   cup quartered artichoke hearts, cut in half
12 small pitted ripe olives, coarsely chopped

1. Preheat oven to 425 degrees.

2. Coat both sides of the tortillas with cooking spray and place on two baking sheets. Bake 3 minutes or until lightly golden on bottom.

3. Remove from heat and spoon sauce evenly over each tortilla. Top with feta, pine nuts, red pepper, basil, artichokes, and olives. Bake 8 to 10 minutes or until slightly golden on edges. Remove from heat and let stand on baking sheets 2 to 3 minutes to firm up slightly.

Cook's Note The tortillas may puff slightly in the first few minutes of baking but will flatten when you add the ingredients.

PER SERVING
Calories: 270
Fat: 12 g
Saturated fat: 3.5 g
Cholesterol: 10 mg
Sodium: 650 mg
Carbohydrate: 10 g
Dietary fiber: 5 g
Sugars: 4 g
Protein: 9 g

Walnut-Arugula Bulgur Bowls

Walnuts are one of the few nuts that don't really need toasting to bring out their natural flavors, so using them as your nut of choice saves a step...just toss them in! They have tons of character, texture, and flavor just as they are.

SERVES 4

1   cup bulgur
1   lemon
    Salt and freshly ground black pepper
½   cup crumbled feta cheese
2   cups arugula
½   cup chopped roasted red peppers
½   cup chopped walnuts

1. Cook bulgur in a medium saucepan according to package directions. Zest the lemon and toss with the bulgur. Season with salt and pepper.

2. Divide the bulgur equally between four shallow bowls. Top with the feta, arugula, roasted red peppers, and walnuts. Cut the lemon into four wedges and serve alongside.

Cook's Note

When grating the lemon rind, grate lightly. You don't want to use the white part (the pith) beneath the lemon rind...it's bitter.

PER SERVING
Calories: 290
Fat: 14 g
Saturated fat: 3 g
Cholesterol: 10 mg
Sodium: 160 mg
Carbohydrate: 36 g
Dietary fiber: 9 g
Sugars: 3 g
Protein: 10 g

Fresh Basil Marinara on Zucchini Ribbons

"Zucchini noodles" can be purchased in the produce section of your supermarket, but it's so easy and fun to make "ribbons" instead. By using a vegetable peeler and running it down the length of the zucchini, delicate, thin ribbons form. The ribbons make a great, super-quick base to top with beans, marinara sauce, feta, basil, and toasted pine nuts!

SERVES 4

- 2 cups reduced-sodium marinara sauce
- ½ cup pine nuts
- 2 zucchini
- 1 (15-ounce) can no-salt-added navy beans, rinsed and drained
- ½ cup crumbled feta cheese
- ¼ cup chopped fresh basil

PER SERVING

Calories: 350
Fat: 20 g
Saturated fat: 3.5 g
Cholesterol: 10 mg
Sodium: 450 mg
Carbohydrate: 33 g
Dietary fiber: 9 g
Sugars: 9 g
Protein: 14 g

1. Place the marinara sauce in a small saucepan over medium heat and cook until heated through. Reduce heat to low and cover to keep warm.

2. Heat a large nonstick skillet over medium-high heat. Add the pine nuts and cook, stirring frequently, for 2 minutes or until beginning to brown lightly. Set aside on separate plate.

3. Using a vegetable peeler, run the peeler down the side of the zucchini lengthwise to create ribbons.

4. Coat zucchini with cooking spray. Heat the skillet over medium-high heat. Add the zucchini and cook, tossing constantly, for 1 minute, or until heated through but not wilted. Reduce heat to medium-low and spread zucchini evenly over the bottom of skillet. Sprinkle evenly with the beans, spoon the marinara sauce over all, and sprinkle with the feta, basil, and pine nuts.

Cook's Note

The heat from the zucchini and marinara will gently warm the beans.

Creamy Butternut Squash & Chickpea Soup

Sneak more veggies, fiber, and vitamin A into your day by puréeing chickpeas and squash to make a thick and creamy "buttercup yellow" soup. The chickpeas take on the flavors of the other ingredients while adding body and richness to the dish.

SERVES 4

1 ½ cups chopped onions
1 (12-ounce) package fresh peeled and cubed butternut squash
1 (15.5-ounce) can chickpeas, rinsed and drained
2 cups water
1 cup whole milk
1 tablespoon sugar
Salt and freshly ground black pepper
½ cup 2 percent plain Greek yogurt

1. Heat a large saucepan coated with cooking spray over medium heat. Add the onions and cook, stirring frequently, for 4 minutes or until beginning to lightly brown on edges. Add the squash, chickpeas, and water. Bring to a boil over high heat, reduce heat, cover, and simmer 20 minutes or until squash is very tender. Remove from heat.

2. Working in batches, purée the squash mixture in a blender. Return to saucepan with the milk and sugar. Place over medium heat, cover, and cook 2 to 3 minutes or until thoroughly heated. Season with salt and pepper. Serve topped with yogurt and sprinkled with black pepper.

Cook's Note As a timesaver, you can find cubed squash in the produce section of most major supermarkets.

PER SERVING
Calories: 240
Fat: 4.5 g
Saturated fat: 1.5 g
Cholesterol: 8 mg
Sodium: 160 mg
Carbohydrate: 40 g
Dietary fiber: 8 g
Sugars: 15 g
Protein: 12 g

Fresh Garlic-Parmesan-Walnut Rotini

This is probably the easiest one-pot recipe ever. Steps (and dirty pots) are spared by cooking in stages. When the pasta is near the end of cooking, broccoli is added to the pasta and they are cooked together. Then the pasta-broccoli mixture is drained and returned to the same pot to mix in the remaining ingredients. How easy is that?

SERVES 4

- 6 ounces whole grain rotini
- 3 cups broccoli florets
- ½ cup chopped walnuts
- 1 garlic clove, minced
- 2 tablespoons extra virgin olive oil
- ¼ cup grated Parmesan cheese, divided use
  Salt and freshly ground black pepper

1. Cook pasta according to package directions, adding broccoli 3 minutes before end of cooking time. Remove from heat, drain well, and return to saucepan.

2. Stir in the walnuts, garlic, olive oil, and 2 tablespoons of the Parmesan. Season with salt and pepper and sprinkle with the remaining cheese.

 Cook's Note The raw garlic is lightly mellowed by the heat of the other ingredients but still carries a bit of punch!

PER SERVING

Calories: 340
Fat: 19 g
Saturated fat: 3 g
Cholesterol: Less than 5 mg
Sodium: 80 mg
Carbohydrate: 37 g
Dietary fiber: 7 g
Sugars: 3 g
Protein: 12 g

Warm Farro-Almond Pilaf with Feta

This delicious pilaf can be served warm or served cold as a grain salad. Farro is a wheat product and is one of the oldest grains. Grown in Italy, it is a great source of protein and fiber. It's very versatile, too. You can use it as you would rice or couscous but it has a chewy texture. A definite conversation starter!

SERVES 4

- 1 cup farro
- ½ cup slivered almonds
- 1 cup chopped onions
- 1 cup thinly sliced carrots
- ½ cup frozen green peas, thawed
- 1 tablespoon extra virgin olive oil
- ¼ teaspoon red pepper flakes
- ½ cup crumbled feta cheese
- Salt and freshly ground black pepper

1. Cook farro according to the package directions.

2. Meanwhile, heat a large nonstick skillet over medium-high heat. Add the almonds and cook for 2 minutes, or until beginning to brown lightly, stirring frequently. Set aside on separate plate.

3. Coat the onions and carrots with cooking spray and cook 8 minutes, or until onions are richly browned on edges and carrots are tender crisp, stirring occasionally. Add the peas and cook 1 minute or until heated through. Remove from the heat.

4. Drain farro, if needed, and stir into the carrot mixture with the almonds, olive oil, red pepper flakes, and feta. Season with salt and pepper.

PER SERVING

Calories: 400

Fat: 16 g

Saturated fat: 3 g

Cholesterol: 10 mg

Sodium: 200 mg

Carbohydrate: 50 g

Dietary fiber: 11 g

Sugars: 5 g

Protein: 14 g

Cook's Note

Be sure to cook the onions and carrots until they are very brown to give an added layer of flavor to the dish!

Veggie & Navy Bean Soup

Serve up this no-chop, colorful bowl of comfort in a flash. Just combine the ingredients, simmer, and serve... knowing there's tons of fiber in every serving!

SERVES 4

- 1 (14-ounce) package frozen peppers and onions
- 2 (14.5-ounce) cans stewed tomatoes
- 2 (16-ounce) cans navy beans, rinsed and drained
- 4 cups water
- 1 tablespoon dried Italian seasoning
- 2 tablespoons extra virgin olive oil
- 2 ounces fresh baby spinach
  Salt and freshly ground black pepper

1. Combine frozen peppers and onions, tomatoes, beans, water, and Italian seasoning in a large saucepan. Bring to a boil, reduce heat, cover, and simmer 25 minutes or until onions are tender.

2. Remove from heat and stir in the oil and spinach. Season with salt and pepper.

Leftovers freeze well for later meals.

PER SERVING
Calories: 220
Fat: 5 g
Saturated fat: 1 g
Cholesterol: 0 mg
Sodium: 430 mg
Carbohydrate: 36 g
Dietary fiber: 11 g
Sugars: 9 g
Protein: 9 g

Pesto & Bread Salad

This energy-saving, time-shaving technique for making homemade croutons works every time! Place the bread cubes in a cold oven, then turn the oven on. By the time the oven reaches the set temperature, the croutons are done!

SERVES 4

4   ounces multigrain bakery bread, chopped
⅔ cup basil pesto
     Zest and juice of 1 lemon
½ (15-ounce) can no-salt-added chickpeas, rinsed and drained (about ¾ cup)
6   cups spring greens or arugula
1   cup halved grape tomatoes or diced fresh tomatoes
     Salt and freshly ground black pepper

1. Place the bread cubes on a baking sheet in a single layer and place in cold oven. Set the oven to 350 degrees and bake 15 minutes, or until lightly browned and slightly firm. Remove from oven and let stand 5 minutes on baking sheet to cool completely and continue to firm up.

2. Combine the pesto and lemon juice and zest in a medium bowl and stir until well blended. Add the bread and chickpeas and toss until well coated.

3. Top lettuce and tomatoes with bread cube mixture and season with salt and pepper.

 Cook's Note Homemade croutons are better for you and taste so much better than store-bought varieties.

PER SERVING
Calories: 290
Fat: 15 g
Saturated fat: 2.5 g
Cholesterol: 6 mg
Sodium: 470 mg
Carbohydrate: 29 g
Dietary fiber: 5 g
Sugars: 5 g
Protein: 10 g

Edamame & Pineapple Grain Medley Bowls

Grain bowls are in demand. Why not add even more flavor and nutritional goodness by using a mixture of quick-cooking grains, such as a multigrain medley of brown, red, and wild rice and quinoa...and cook it with edamame! Top it with a splash of soy sauce and sections of green onion, toasted almonds, and sweet pineapple.

SERVES 4

- 1 cup slivered almonds
- 2 (3-ounce) packages multigrain medley
- 1 cup frozen or fresh shelled edamame
- ¼ cup reduced-sodium soy sauce
- 1⅓ cups chopped pineapple or mango, fresh or frozen and thawed
- ½ cup chopped green onion
- ¼ cup chopped fresh cilantro, optional

1. Heat a large skillet over medium-high heat. Add the almonds and cook 2 minutes or until beginning to brown lightly, stirring frequently. Set aside on separate plate.

2. Place multigrain mixture and edamame in the skillet and cook according to multigrain package directions.

3. Divide the edamame-multigrain mixture evenly between four bowls. Spoon the soy sauce over all and top with the almonds, pineapple, and green onions. Sprinkle with cilantro, if desired.

 Cook's Note The multigrain medley can be found in the rice aisle of your supermarket.

PER SERVING

Calories: 430

Fat: 19 g

Saturated fat: 1.5 g

Cholesterol: 0 mg

Sodium: 570 mg

Carbohydrate: 54 g

Dietary fiber: 9 g

Sugars: 10 g

Protein: 16 g

Kitchen Measurements & Metric Conversion Chart

COMMON KITCHEN MEASUREMENTS

1 gallon = 4 quarts = 8 pints = 16 cups

1 quart = 2 pints = 4 cups

1 pint = 2 cups

1 cup = 16 tablespoons

¼ cup = 4 tablespoons = 12 teaspoons

1 tablespoon = 3 teaspoons

METRIC EQUIVALENTS, WEIGHT

0.35 ounce	1 gram
¼ ounce	7 grams
½ ounce	14 grams
¾ ounce	21 grams
1 ounce	28 grams
1 ½ ounces	42.5 grams
2 ounces	57 grams
3 ounces	85 grams
4 ounces	113 grams
5 ounces	142 grams
6 ounces	170 grams
7 ounces	198 grams
8 ounces	227 grams
16 ounces (1 pound)	454 grams
2.2 pounds	1 kilogram

METRIC EQUIVALENTS, VOLUME

(ml=milliliter)

¼ teaspoon	1 ml
½ teaspoon	2.5 ml
¾ teaspoon	4 ml
1 teaspoon	5 ml
1 ¼ teaspoon	6 ml
1 ½ teaspoon	7.5 ml
1 ¾ teaspoon	8.5 ml
2 teaspoons	10 ml
1 tablespoon	15 ml
2 tablespoons	30 ml
¼ cup	59 ml
⅓ cup	79 ml
½ cup	118 ml
⅔ cup	158 ml
¾ cup	178 ml
1 cup	237 ml
1 ½ cups	355 ml
2 cups (1 pint)	473 ml
3 cups	710 ml
4 cups (1 quart)	.95 liter
1.06 quarts	1 liter
4 quarts (1 gallon)	3.8 liters

About the American Cancer Society

The American Cancer Society is a nationwide, community-based voluntary health organization dedicated to eliminating cancer as a major health problem. Our mission is to save lives, celebrate lives, and lead the fight for a world without cancer. For more information, please visit **cancer.org**.

About the American Cancer Society Book Publishing Program

We are the world's leading publisher of consumer books on cancer, focusing on caregiving, family support, coping, and managing the side effects of cancer treatment. Our books are winners of more than 100 awards for content and design excellence.

In addition to books on cancer, we also publish cookbooks focused on prevention. Based on our Guidelines for Nutrition and Physical Activity for Cancer Prevention, our cookbooks are centered on building healthy eating habits to help people reduce their risk of chronic diseases, such as cancer, heart disease, and diabetes.

For more information about all our books, visit **cancer.org/bookstore.**

Other Cookbooks from the American Cancer Society

The American Cancer Society New Healthy Eating Cookbook, Fourth Edition

Maya's Secrets: Delightful Latin Dishes for a Healthier You

Los Secretos de Maya: Deliciosas Recetas Latinas para una Buena Salud

What to Eat During Cancer Treatment, Second Edition

For more information about all our books, visit **cancer.org/bookstore**.